the dalai lama
on the epistle of james

with an introduction by the

dalai lama

authorised king james bible

printed by authority

published by canongate

First published in Great Britain in 2000
by Canongate Books Ltd
14 High Street, Edinburgh EH1 1TE

10 9 8 7 6 5 4 3 2 1

Introduction copyright © His Holiness the Dalai Lama
of Tibet, 2000
The moral right of the author has been asserted

British Library Cataloguing-in-Publication Data
A catalogue record is available on request from
the British Library

ISBN 0 86241 975 1

Typeset by Palimpsest Book Production
Book design by Paddy Cramsie at et al
Printed and bound in Great Britain by Omnia

a note about pocket canons

The Authorised King James Version of the Bible, translated between 1604–11, coincided with an extraordinary flowering of English literature. This version, more than any other, and possibly more than any other work in history, has had an influence in shaping the language we speak and write today.

Twenty-seven of the eighty original books of the King James Bible are brought to you in this series. They encompass categories as diverse as history, philosophy, law, poetry and fiction. Each Pocket Canon also has its own introduction, specially commissioned from an impressive range of writers, to provide a personal interpretation of the text and explore its contemporary relevance.

introduction by his holiness the dalai lama

His Holiness the 14th Dalai Lama, Tenzin Gyatso, is the head of state and spiritual leader of the Tibetan people. He was born in 1935 to a peasant family and recognised as the reincarnation of the 13th Dalai Lama at the age of two. He began his monastic Buddhist education when he was six. 'Dalai Lama' is a Mongolian title meaning 'Ocean of Wisdom'. In 1959 he was forced into exile with the brutal suppression of the Tibetan National Uprising in Lhasa by Chinese troops. For the last 39 years he has been living in Dharamsala, India. As leader of the Tibetan Government-in-Exile he advocates democracy and autonomy for the Tibetan people from Chinese rule. In his lectures and tours around the world he emphasises the importance of love, compassion and forgiveness. His publications in English include Ancient Wisdom Modern World *and his autobiography* Freedom in Exile. *His Holiness was awarded the Nobel Prize for Peace in 1989.*

As I read the lines of this *Epistle of James*, I am struck by the similarities between this beautiful letter in the Bible and some of the texts in my own Buddhist tradition, especially those that belong to a genre known as *lojong*, literally meaning 'training the mind'. As with *lojong* texts, I believe, this epistle can be read on different levels. On the practical level, however, it encapsulates many of the key principles that are crucial for learning how to be a better human being. More precisely, it teaches us how to bring our spiritual vision to life at the highest possible level.

I feel humbled to be invited to write an introduction to this important part of the Christian scriptures. As we enter a new millennium and Christians all over the world celebrate two thousand years of their tradition, I am reminded that this holy scripture has been a powerful source of spiritual inspiration and solace to millions of fellow human beings world-wide. Needless to say, I am no expert on Christian scriptures. I have, however, accepted the invitation to comment personally on the epistle from the perspective of my own Buddhist tradition. I will particularly focus on passages that evoke values and principles also emphasised in the Buddhist scriptures.

The epistle begins by underlining the critical importance of developing a single-pointed commitment to our chosen spiritual path. It says, 'A double minded man is unstable in all his ways' (James 1:8), because lack of commitment and a wavering mind are among the greatest obstacles to a successful spiritual life. However, this need not be some kind of blind faith, but rather a commitment based on personal appreciation of the value and efficacy of the spiritual path. Such faith arises through a process of reflection and deep understanding. Buddhist texts describe three levels of faith, namely: faith as admiration, faith as reasoned conviction, and faith as emulation of high spiritual ideals. I believe that these three kinds of faith are applicable here as well.

The epistle reminds us of the power of the destructive tendencies that exist naturally in all of us. In what is, for me at least, the most poignant verse of the entire letter, we read, 'Wherefore, my beloved brethren, let every man be swift to hear, slow to speak, slow to wrath: for the wrath of man worketh not the righteousness of God' (James 1:19-20).

These two verses encapsulate principles that are of utmost importance to a spiritual practitioner, and for that matter, any individual who aspires to express his or her basic human goodness. This emphasis on hearing as opposed to speaking teaches us the need for open-heartedness. For without it we have no room to receive the blessings and positive transformation that we might otherwise experience in our interaction with our fellow human beings.

Open and receptive, swift to listen to others, we

should be slow to speak, because speech is a powerful instrument that can be highly constructive or profoundly destructive. We are all aware how seemingly harmless speech can actually inflict deep hurt upon others. Therefore, the wise course is to follow the advice of one well-known Buddhist *lojong* text: 'When amongst many, guard your speech and alone, guard your thoughts.'

The instruction that we should be 'slow to wrath' reminds us that it is vital to ensure some degree of restraint over powerful negative emotions like anger, for actions motivated by such states of mind are almost invariably destructive. This is something we must both appreciate and strive to implement in our everyday lives. Only then can we hope to reap the fruit of living a spiritual life.

The real test of spiritual practice lies in the practitioner's behaviour. There is sometimes a tendency to think of the spiritual life as primarily introspective, divorced from the concerns of everyday life and society. This, I believe, is plainly wrong and is also rejected in this epistle. Faith that does not translate into actions is no faith at all, as the text says:

> If a brother or sister be naked, and destitute of daily food, and any of you say unto them, 'Depart in peace, be ye warmed and filled'; notwithstanding ye give them not those things which are needful to the body; what doth it profit? Even so faith, if it hath not works, is dead, being alone (James 2:16-17).

We find a similar principle in Buddhist texts as well. They advise that when helping others, giving material aid comes first, speaking words of comfort comes second, giving spiritual counsel comes third, while fourth is demonstrating what you teach by your own personal example.

I have long been an admirer of the Christian tradition of charity and social work. The image of monks and nuns devoting their entire lives to the service of humanity in the fields of health, education and care of the poor is truly inspiring. To me, these are true followers of Christ, demonstrating their faith in compassionate action.

The epistle addresses what a Buddhist might call 'contemplation of the transient nature of life.' This is beautifully captured in the following verse: 'Whereas ye know not what shall be on the morrow. For what is your life? It is even a vapour, that appeareth for a little time, and then vanisheth away' (James 4:24).

In the Buddhist context, contemplation of life's transient nature brings a sense of urgency to our spiritual life. We may be aware of the value of spiritual practice, but in our daily lives, we tend to behave as if we will live for a long time. We have a false sense of the permanence of our existence, which is one of the greatest obstacles to a dedicated spiritual life. More important, from an ethical point of view, it is the assumption of permanence that leads us to pursue what we see as the 'legitimate' desires and needs of our enduring 'self'. We ignore the impact of our behaviour on other people's lives. We might even be willing to exploit others for our own ends. So, profound contemplation of life's transient nature introduces a note of healthy realism into our life as it helps put things in proper perspective.

The epistle is passionate in its advocacy of respect for the poor. In fact, it presents a severe critique of the conceit and complacency of the rich and the powerful. Some of these criticisms may have a certain historical significance, but they underline an important spiritual principle, which is never to forget the fundamental equality of all human beings. A true spiritual practitioner appreciates what I often describe as our 'basic spirituality'. By this I am referring to the fundamental qualities of goodness, which exist naturally in all of us irrespective of our gender, race, social and religious backgrounds.

By criticising disdainful attitudes towards the poor, the epistle persuasively reminds us of the need to return to a deeper appreciation of our humanity. It reminds us to relate to fellow human beings at a level of basic humanity. I often tell people that when I meet someone for the first time, my primary feeling is that I am meeting a fellow human being. It does not matter to me, whether the person is considered 'important' or not. For me, what matters most is basic warm-heartedness.

Certainly, from the standpoint of mere humanity, there are no grounds for discrimination. In the language of the Bible, we are all equal in the face of creation. And in the language of Buddhism, we all equally aspire for happiness and shun suffering. Furthermore, we all have the right to fulfil this basic aspiration to be happy and overcome suffering. So if we truly relate to our fellow human beings with a recognition of our fundamental equality, considerations of whether someone is rich or poor, educated or uneducated, black or white, male or female, or whether he or she belongs to this or that religion naturally become secondary.

When we read this text from the Bible today, two thousand years after it was written, it reminds us that not only are many of our fundamental spiritual values universal, they are also perennial. So long as human beings' fundamental nature, aspiring for happiness and wishing to overcome suffering, remains unchanged, these basic values too will remain relevant to us both as individual human beings and as a society.

I would like to conclude by remembering my

friend Thomas Merton, a Catholic monk of the Cistercian order, who opened my eyes to the richness of the Christian tradition. It is to him that I owe my first, real appreciation of the value of Christian teachings. Since we met in the early 1960s, I have dedicated a large part of my time and effort to promoting deeper understanding amongst the followers of the world's major religions. And it is to this noble objective that I dedicate the words I have written here.

the general epistle of james

James, a servant of God and of the Lord Jesus Christ,
to the twelve tribes which are scattered abroad,
greeting.

² My brethren, count it all joy
   when ye fall into divers temptations;
³ knowing this, that the trying of your faith
   worketh patience.
⁴ But let patience have her perfect work,
   that ye may be perfect and entire,
      wanting nothing.

⁵ If any of you lack wisdom,
   let him ask of God,
      that giveth to all men liberally,

and upbraideth not;

　　and it shall be given him.

⁶ But let him ask in faith, nothing wavering.

　　For he that wavereth

　　　is like a wave of the sea

　　driven with the wind and tossed.

⁷ For let not that man think

　　that he shall receive

　　　any thing of the Lord.

⁸ A double minded man is unstable

　　in all his ways.

⁹ Let the brother of low degree

　　rejoice in that he is exalted:

¹⁰ but the rich, in that he is made low,

　　because as the flower of the grass

　　　he shall pass away.

¹¹ For the sun is no sooner risen

　　with a burning heat,

but it withereth the grass,

and the flower thereof falleth,

and the grace of

the fashion of it perisheth:

so also shall the rich man

fade away in his ways.

¹² Blessed is the man

that endureth temptation,

for when he is tried,

he shall receive the crown of life,

which the Lord hath promised

to them that love him.

¹³ Let no man say when he is tempted,

I am tempted of God,

for God cannot be tempted with evil,

neither tempteth he any man.

¹⁴ But every man is tempted,

when he is drawn away

of his own lust, and enticed.

¹⁵ Then when lust hath conceived,
   it bringeth forth sin:
     and sin, when it is finished,
   bringeth forth death.

¹⁶ Do not err, my beloved brethren.

¹⁷ Every good gift and every perfect gift
   is from above,
     and cometh down
   from the Father of lights,
     with whom is no variableness,
   neither shadow of turning.

¹⁸ Of his own will begat he us
   with the word of truth,
     that we should be a kind of
   firstfruits of his creatures.

¹⁹ Wherefore, my beloved brethren,

let every man be swift to hear,

slow to speak, slow to wrath,

²⁰ for the wrath of man worketh not

the righteousness of God.

²¹ Wherefore lay apart all filthiness

and superfluity of naughtiness,

and receive with meekness

the engrafted word,

which is able to save your souls.

²² But be ye doers of the word,

and not hearers only,

deceiving your own selves.

²³ For if any be a hearer of the word,

and not a doer, he is like unto a man

beholding his natural face in a glass,

²⁴ for he beholdeth himself,

and goeth his way,

and straightway forgetteth

what manner of man he was.

²⁵ But whoso looketh into

the perfect law of liberty,

and continueth therein,

he being not a forgetful hearer,

but a doer of the work,

this man shall be blessed in his deed.

²⁶ If any man among you

seem to be religious,

and bridleth not his tongue,

but deceiveth his own heart,

this man's religion is vain.

²⁷ Pure religion and undefiled

before God and the Father is this:

to visit the fatherless and widows

in their affliction,

and to keep himself unspotted

from the world.

2 My brethren, have not the faith
    of our Lord Jesus Christ,
        the Lord of glory,
    with respect of persons.
² For if there come unto your assembly
    a man with a gold ring,
        in goodly apparel,
    and there come in also a poor man
        in vile raiment;
³ and ye have respect to him
    that weareth the gay clothing,
        and say unto him,
    'Sit thou here in a good place';
        and say to the poor,
    'Stand thou there', or
        'sit here under my footstool',
⁴ are ye not then partial in yourselves,
    and are become judges of evil thoughts?
⁵ Hearken, my beloved brethren,

hath not God chosen

the poor of this world rich in faith,

and heirs of the kingdom

which he hath promised

to them that love him?

6 But ye have despised the poor.

Do not rich men oppress you,

and draw you before

the judgment seats?

7 Do not they blaspheme that worthy name

by the which ye are called?

8 If ye fulfil the royal law

according to the scripture,

'Thou shalt love thy neighbour

as thyself', ye do well,

9 but if ye have respect to persons,

ye commit sin,

and are convinced of the law

as transgressors.

¹⁰ For whosoever shall keep the whole law,

and yet offend in one point,

he is guilty of all.

¹¹ For he that said,

'Do not commit adultery',

said also, 'Do not kill.'

Now if thou commit no adultery,

yet if thou kill,

thou art become a transgressor of the law.

¹² So speak ye, and so do,

as they that shall be judged

by the law of liberty.

¹³ For he shall have judgment without mercy,

that hath shewed no mercy;

and mercy rejoiceth against judgment.

¹⁴ What doth it profit, my brethren,

though a man say he hath faith,

and have not works?

Can faith save him?

¹⁵ If a brother or sister be naked,

and destitute of daily food,

¹⁶ and one of you say unto them,

'Depart in peace,

be ye warmed and filled',

notwithstanding ye give them not

those things which are needful

to the body; what doth it profit?

¹⁷ Even so faith, if it hath not works,

is dead, being alone.

¹⁸ Yea, a man may say,

'Thou hast faith, and I have works':

shew me thy faith without thy works,

and I will shew thee my faith

by my works.

¹⁹ Thou believest that there is one God;

thou doest well:

the devils also believe, and tremble.

²⁰ But wilt thou know, O vain man,

that faith without works is dead?

²¹ Was not Abraham our father

justified by works,

when he had offered Isaac his son

upon the altar?

²² Seest thou how faith

wrought with his works,

and by works was faith made perfect?

²³ And the scripture was fulfilled

which saith, 'Abraham believed God,

and it was imputed unto him

for righteousness':

and he was called the Friend of God.

²⁴ Ye see then how that by works

a man is justified, and not by faith only.

²⁵ Likewise also was not Rahab
 the harlot justified by works,
  when she had received the messengers,
 and had sent them out another way?
²⁶ For as the body without the spirit is dead,
 so faith without works is dead also.

3 My brethren, be not many masters,
knowing that we shall receive
the greater condemnation.
² For in many things we offend all.
If any man offend not in word,
the same is a perfect man,
and able also to bridle the whole body.
³ Behold, we put bits in the horses' mouths,
that they may obey us;
and we turn about their whole body.
⁴ Behold also the ships,
which though they be so great,
and are driven of fierce winds,
yet are they turned about
with a very small helm,
whithersoever the governor listeth.

⁵ Even so the tongue is a little member,
and boasteth great things.

Behold, how great a matter
a little fire kindleth!
⁶And the tongue is a fire,
a world of iniquity:
so is the tongue among our members,
that it defileth the whole body,
and setteth on fire the course of nature;
and it is set on fire of hell.
⁷For every kind of beasts,
and of birds, and of serpents,
and of things in the sea, is tamed,
and hath been tamed of mankind,
⁸but the tongue can no man tame;
it is an unruly evil,
full of deadly poison.
⁹Therewith bless we God, even the Father;
and therewith curse we men,
which are made after the similitude
of God.

¹⁰ Out of the same mouth proceedeth
    blessing and cursing.
        My brethren, these things
    ought not so to be.
¹¹ Doth a fountain send forth
    at the same place
        sweet water and bitter?
¹² Can the fig tree, my brethren,
    bear olive berries?
        Either a vine, figs?
    So can no fountain both yield
        salt water and fresh.

¹³ Who is a wise man
    and endued with knowledge among you?
        Let him shew
    out of a good conversation
        his works with meekness of wisdom.
¹⁴ But if ye have bitter envying

and strife in your hearts, glory not,
and lie not against the truth.

¹⁵ This wisdom descendeth not from above,
but is earthly, sensual, devilish.

¹⁶ For where envying and strife is,
there is confusion and every evil work.

¹⁷ But the wisdom that is from above
is first pure, then peaceable,
gentle, and easy to be intreated,
full of mercy and good fruits,
without partiality,
and without hypocrisy.

¹⁸ And the fruit of righteousness
is sown in peace of them that make peace.

4 From whence come wars
and fightings among you?
Come they not hence,
even of your lusts
that war in your members?
² Ye lust, and have not:
ye kill, and desire to have,
and cannot obtain:
ye fight and war, yet ye have not,
because ye ask not.
³ Ye ask, and receive not,
because ye ask amiss,
that ye may consume it
upon your lusts.
⁴ Ye adulterers and adulteresses,
know ye not
that the friendship of the world
is enmity with God?
Whosoever therefore will be

a friend of the world

    is the enemy of God.

⁵ Do ye think that the scripture saith in vain,

    'The spirit that dwelleth in us

lusteth to envy'?

⁶ But he giveth more grace.

Wherefore he saith,

    'God resisteth the proud,

but giveth grace unto the humble.'

⁷ Submit yourselves therefore to God.

Resist the devil,

    and he will flee from you.

⁸ Draw nigh to God,

and he will draw nigh to you.

    Cleanse your hands, ye sinners;

and purify your hearts,

    ye double minded.

⁹ Be afflicted, and mourn, and weep:

let your laughter be turned to mourning,

and your joy to heaviness.
¹⁰ Humble yourselves in the sight of the Lord,
and he shall lift you up.

¹¹ Speak not evil one of another, brethren.
He that speak-eth evil of his brother,
and judgeth his brother,
speaketh evil of the law,
and judgeth the law:
but if thou judge the law,
thou art not a doer of the law,
but a judge.
¹² There is one lawgiver,
who is able to save and to destroy:
who art thou that judgest another?

¹³ Go to now, ye that say,
'Today or tomorrow
we will go into such a city,

and continue there a year,

and buy and sell, and get gain,

¹⁴ whereas ye know not

what shall be on the morrow.

For what is your life?

It is even a vapour,

that appeareth for a little time,

and then vanisheth away.

¹⁵ For that ye ought to say,

'If the Lord will, we shall live,

and do this, or that.'

¹⁶ But now ye rejoice in your boastings:

all such rejoicing is evil.

¹⁷ Therefore to him that knoweth to do good,

and doeth it not,

to him it is sin.

5 Go to now, ye rich men,

weep and howl for your miseries

that shall come upon you.

² Your riches are corrupted,

and your garments are motheaten.

³ Your gold and silver is cankered;

and the rust of them

shall be a witness against you,

and shall eat your flesh as it were fire.

Ye have heaped treasure together

for the last days.

⁴ Behold, the hire of the labourers

who have reaped down your fields,

which is of you

kept back by fraud, crieth:

and the cries of them

which have reaped are entered

into the ears of the Lord of sabaoth.

⁵ Ye have lived in pleasure on the earth,

and been wanton;

ye have nourished your hearts,

as in a day of slaughter.

⁶ Ye have condemned and killed the just;

and he doth not resist you.

⁷ Be patient therefore, brethren,

unto the coming of the Lord.

Behold, the husbandman waiteth

for the precious fruit of the earth,

and hath long patience for it,

until he receive the early and latter rain.

⁸ Be ye also patient; stablish your hearts,

for the coming of the Lord draweth nigh.

⁹ Grudge not one against another, brethren,

lest ye be condemned:

behold, the judge standeth

before the door.

¹⁰ Take, my brethren, the prophets,

who have spoken in the name of the Lord,

for an example of suffering affliction,

and of patience.

¹¹ Behold, we count them happy

which endure.

Ye have heard of the patience of Job,

and have seen the end of the Lord;

that the Lord is very pitiful,

and of tender mercy.

¹² But above all things, my brethren,

swear not,

neither by heaven,

neither by the earth,

neither by any other oath;

but let your yea be yea;

and your nay, nay;

lest ye fall into condemnation.

¹³ Is any among you afflicted?

Let him pray.

Is any merry?

Let him sing psalms.

¹⁴ Is any sick among you?

Let him call for the elders of the church;

and let them pray over him,

anointing him with oil

in the name of the Lord,

¹⁵ and the prayer of faith shall save the sick,

and the Lord shall raise him up;

and if he have committed sins,

they shall be forgiven him.

¹⁶ Confess your faults one to another,

and pray one for another,

that ye may be healed.

The effectual fervent prayer

of a righteous man availeth much.

¹⁷ Elias was a man

subject to like passions as we are,

and he prayed earnestly

that it might not rain:

and it rained not on the earth

by the space of three years and six months.

¹⁸And he prayed again,

and the heaven gave rain,

and the earth brought forth her fruit.

¹⁹Brethren, if any of you do err

from the truth,

and one convert him;

²⁰let him know,

that he which converteth the sinner

from the error of his way

shall save a soul from death,

and shall hide a multitude of sins.

other books in the pocket canon series

Genesis – introduced by Steven Rose
0 86241 789 9   £1.00

Exodus – introduced by David Grossman
0 86241 790 2   £1.00

Ruth & Esther – introduced by Joanna Trollope
0 86241 968 9   £1.50

Samuel I & II – introduced by Meir Shalev
0 86241 967 0   £1.50

Job – introduced by Louis de Bernières
0 86241 791 0   £1.00

Psalms – introduced by Bono
0 86241 969 7   £1.50

Proverbs – introduced by Charles Johnson
0 86241 792 9   £1.00

Ecclesiastes – introduced by Doris Lessing
0 86241 794 5   £1.00

Song of Solomon – introduced by A S Byatt
0 86241 793 7   £1.00

Isaiah – introduced by Peter Ackroyd
0 86241 970 0   £1.50

Jonah, Micah & Nahum – introduced by Alasdair Gray
0 86241 971 9   £1.50

Wisdom – introduced by Piers Paul Read
0 86241 980 8   £1.50

Matthew – introduced by A N Wilson
0 86241 795 3   £1.00

Mark – introduced by Nick Cave
0 86241 796 1   £1.00

Luke – introduced by Richard Holloway
0 86241 797 X   £1.00

John – introduced by Blake Morrison
0 86241 798 8   £1.00

Acts – introduced by P D James
0 86241 973 5   £1.50

Romans – introduced by Ruth Rendell
0 86241 972 7   £1.50

Corinthians I & II – introduced by Fay Weldon
0 86241 799 6   £1.00

Hebrews – introduced by Karen Armstrong
0 86241 974 3   £1.50

Revelation – introduced by Will Self
0 86241 800 3   £1.00

All of the above titles can be ordered in box sets:

Set One – Genesis, Exodus, Job, Proverbs,
Ecclesiastes, Song of Solomon,
Matthew, Mark, Luke, John,
Corinthians I & II, Revelation
0 86241 861 5   £12.99

Set Two – Ruth & Esther, Samuel I & II,
Psalms, Isaiah, Jonah Micah & Nahum,
Wisdom, Acts, Romans, Hebrews
0 86241 963 8   £12.99

Orders can be made directly to:
Canongate Books Ltd,
14 High Street,
Edinburgh EH1 1TE
Tel 0131 557 5111
Fax 0131 557 5211
or via our web-site at
www.canongate.net/canons